The Other Side of The Wall

**How to Survive Your
Loved One's Incarceration**

By Sharon Brooks Green

By Sharon Brooks Green

Printed in the United States of America

First Printing, 2019

ISBN 978-0-359-86059-3

Formatted by Show Your Success

Edited & Published by SBG

Introduction

First my brother went to prison. As I got older I realized that he was actually not the first, but the first one that I remember.

My Mother would often meet in our kitchen with her beloved Mother, her sisters, cousins, older daughters and female neighbors. Together they discussed the situation of my brother being 'behind the wall'. They all sympathized with her, bringing food, beer and always good cheer.

My brother got plenty of letters from the ladies. They wrote him right there at our kitchen table. Even though I was a kid, I always got my letter in too! Occasionally he would receive a whole $5 bill from somebody, (no JPay back then). He would even get a Polaroid picture or two. Pictures of our large family and our pets. He really liked our pet dog Ajax, so my Mother made sure he got some pictures of him.

My Grandmother didn't smoke, but almost all of the other women did. There were Winstons, Kents and Virginia Slims smoke throughout the house. I thought they all looked so cool, really sophisticated. It's still amazing to me that I never became a smoker.

As together as these women were, occasionally they would cry. I saw them smile a lot too. They would pray out of nowhere! Then go right back to smiling and laughing for a while. You see, mass incarceration did not exist in the Black community yet, so my brother being in jail/prison was uncommon amongst them. Him being in prison was a big thing. A serious matter.

Eventually, somebody would put on the music and the Men, (most of them smoked Kool's), would join in from the backyard. I didn't sit in on their gatherings, but I know they discussed my brother. When they came in everybody enjoyed the soul music together. A lot of love in the room. The music of Marvin Gaye, Al Green, Minnie Riperton, The Jackson 5, Aretha Franklin, Diana Ross, James Brown, Stevie Wonder, LOTS of Jazz music and sometimes Billie Holiday along with many, many other soul-singing greats. The music seemed to make everybody happy. Peace and hope for the future was in the air.

About once a month, some of them would get in the car with my Mother and go visit my brother. As the youngest daughter, I was often in the car with her, listening....learning.

25 years later, I was the Mother and the imprisoned was my Son.

This introduction is the true origin of this book.

I wrote "The Other Side of the Wall: Surviving Your Loved One's Incarceration" for anyone who is experiencing the life-changing situation of having someone you know imprisoned. I founded my non-profit Peace of Hope, Inc. based on the same premises.

This book focuses on YOU and your well-being and gives realistic tools on surviving the other side of the wall.

Sharon Brooks Green
Author

Dedication

With unmatched loyalty, I dedicate this book to
Almighty God.

By His mercy and grace, I am a survivor. Amen.

Table of Contents

Acknowledgements

- Peace of Hope, Inc.
- The Brooks Family
- The Wingfield Family
- The Green Family
- MAPL (and student club APLS)
- Rotary Club of Crystal-New Hope-Robbinsdale
- Rotary Club of North Minneapolis
- Hennepin Healthcare
- Minneapolis Urban League
- KMOJ FM 89.9
- Zion Temple Missionary Baptist Church, IL
- Shiloh Temple International Ministries, MN
- New Salem M.B. Church, MN
- Episcopal Church of MN Executive Offices
- Community Partnership Collaborative 2.0
- MN Spokesman Recorder
- Twin Cities Radio Network (TCRN)
- EMERGE Career & Technology Center
- Insight News
- Mr. CleanHouse Productions
- 10 Glamchildren & 1 GreatGlamchild
- CCX Media
- Pioneer Press
- Northside Economic Opportunity Network(NEON)
- Oak Park Comm. Center(Pillsbury United Communities)
- Professor Mahmoud El-Kati
- Kelis Houston
- Kerry Jo Felder
- Linnetta Gilmore Coleman
- Annette Butler-Bryant
- Myron B. Green

Acknowledgements

- Cynthia Jackson
- Taurea V. Avant
- Kimuel Hailey
- M.J. Lavigne
- Lee Buckley
- Anthony Tunstall
- MN Department of Corrections
- U.S.A. Public Library System
- Cookie Cart
- Sophia Lorraine Crosby
- The McDonald's Corporation
- Mrs. Mary Frances Burkley
- NAACP
- Donald Jackson
- MicroGrants
- Tiffini Flynn Forslund
- Blair Lee
- Sammy's Avenue Eatery
- Authors of MN Bills HF 4151 & 1518 (& SF Companions)
- Ms. Patricia "Patti" Holmes
- Marcia Haffmans
- Ohenewaa Healing Point
- Ride for Love, LLC
- Metropolitan State University, MN
- Inver Hills Community College, MN
- Candace Taylor Anderson
- Deborah Gray
- Dwane E. Martin
- John Turnipseed
- Yenenesh B. Kibrat
- Cecelia Viel
- Marquis, Lawrence & Kamouri
- David Boehnke
- 89th May Street
- FaceBook, Twitter, Instagram, Google & other social media outlets

CHAPTER 1

Stay In The Moment

"Life gives you plenty of time to do whatever you want to do if you stay in the present moment."

— Deepak Chopra

The phone rings and in retrospect, it seems like it rung differently that time. It's a call that no one wants to hear: "This is a call from a correctional facility…"
And at that moment your world is completely changed.

Depending on the circumstances, the moment could be short-lived or last for a very long time. In either time frame, you as the support person of the detained must still survive! Which brings us to our title "The Other Side of the Wall".

Prison (and other detention facilities) has long associated those inside as being 'behind the wall'. Thus, you the supporter, are on the other side of the wall.

This is no easy assignment! Staying in the moment is paramount to survival during this predicament.

This chapter is dedicated to equipping you with the tools to remain useful and not overwhelmed, in this new situation.

For many of you, this situation is not new. You may recognize these tools and that is good. Use this book as a reminder to what surviving on the other side of the wall feels like. Be invigorated.

PAY ATTENTION TO YOUR THOUGHTS and WORDS

Good thoughts, not so good thoughts, random thoughts and the intense ones, they all matter. It is often said that thoughts become actions, but usually it's thoughts become words then words become actions.

What we think, say and do (as used in The Rotary Club's 4-Way Test) and how we respond to this mantra of good, can have an overwhelmingly positive outcome for ourselves and those we support. It is important to give authentic answers to yourself when choosing to support an imprisoned loved one.

Your role as a support person of someone detained is only as effective as how you treat yourself.

Life can be busy and actions can become methodical. You can get used to doing everyday duties and saying things you've either have always said or things that have been accepted into your understanding and is now routine.

However, while communicating to someone whose routine consist of strict routine, protocols and security, your thoughts which turns into words and sometimes move into actions, must be controlled.

Here are some phrases to detox from your vocabulary:

"I'm doin' time with you".

"There's nothing I can do".

"I don't know what I'll do if ...".

"My life has no meaning until you get out".

"I refuse to have fun while you're behind bars".

"While you are behind the wall, you no longer exist to me".

These phrases stem from self-destructive thoughts and can take on a down-hill spiral of actions in life.

Thoughts such as these may come in spurts like revelations as you encounter a variety of situations. Often, there is no one to share these thoughts with or worse, you share your thoughts with someone and they cannot relate. Some may want to 'change the subject' or 'gloss over the topic' as if it were not worthy even to talk about, leaving you stuck with the negative thought basically still there. Friends may label you as 'emotional' or may determine that you're 'all over the place', but know for yourself that your thoughts and words ARE important. No need to force that situation, move on.

Note: Imprisonment is not an easy topic.

Living on the other side of the wall can be a challenging time. The thoughts we come up with may be sound and clear or irrational and uncommon, all of them are relevant to shaping you into the best support person you can be for yourself and for your loved one who is now detained.

Pay strict attention to your thoughts and words during this time.

Relax. Think. Review. Speak.

Review Your Thoughts Concerning the Situation

e.g. You got 'the call'. Your Daughter was arrested. You went to court with her every time. She got convicted of a felony. Time in jail – 4 months. Prison time 2 years. 1 more to go. You are angry at the choices she made. You feel ashamed, even guilty concerning your parenting skills. She has apologized to you. She sends birthday and holiday cards. You cry. Society says bad things about her.

You visit. You naturally love her anyhow. So you go to work with your head up. You are not 'doing time with her', you're living your life as best you can. So is she. Life continues for both of you. Soon this will be a life lesson of the past.

Your thoughts set the pace on how you *maintain* survival throughout the incarceration of your loved one.

If it comes down to speaking out loud what you are thinking to yourself —just do it! Hear the words. Determine whether or not they are healthy. You decide. Don't brush your thoughts off because what <u>you</u> think is *very* important. Your closest friend may agree and listen. That is good. A therapist is not a bad idea at this time either.

Once you are able to review your thoughts, as in the example given, you will be able to change your words because now, it won't match the negative thoughts. Your thoughts control your words and your words have great effect on your actions. Again, relax, think, review then speak.

Result: Potential positive actions while surviving the other side of the wall.

Try these positive thoughts:

"I love my imprisoned daughter (son, father, mother, sister, brother, friend, etc.)."
"Fighting for his release is important to me, so I know I must remain healthy."
"I support my incarcerated loved one because I want to, not because I have to."

The devastation of knowing that stone walls separate you and your loved one can be extremely hard to bear.

It becomes a necessity to acknowledge the pain, not ignore it. Next, add positive thoughts to accompany pain and the subsequent action (or non-action) that you may take. This kind of exercise becomes transferrable to the person incarcerated. A higher-level of communication between the two of you during visits (phone calls, letters and in-person) may be a result of utilizing the skill of choosing thoughts, words and action.

FEED YOUR FIVE SENSES

Sight, Sound, Scent, Touch & Taste need you to cue them in to this new situation.

Suggestions: If you decide to visit your loved one in a prison or other detention facility, allow your eyes to take in the *sight* of the architectural design of the building. Is it a singular building or comprised of more than one? With real curiosity, use your voice to ask what the buildings are used for. Listen to the *sound* of your tone. Be conscious of the words you use to inquire. Notice the landscape. Are there trees and flowers? Notice the *scent*. Perhaps the visit is via video, acknowledge the *touch* screen as part of the experience. That evening, be conscious of the *taste* of your dinner. Ask your detained loved one to share their 'senses' experiences with you.

While going through the dilemma of knowing that someone you have a close relationship with lives under lock and key, your natural five senses are usually heightened or lowered, rarely do they remain the same. Acknowledge that. Recognize where you are with your senses then challenge yourself to feed your senses differently, like the suggestions above.

Instead of accepting that you have 'lost your appetite', try preparing your food a new way. The 'usual' way may have a negative mental connection to many painful memories. Or perhaps your sense of taste is ready to elevate just like you are! Most of us become acutely aware when one (or more) of the senses becomes altered. This is not unusual especially when faced with extraordinary circumstances such as the new role you now voluntarily carry.

Since we rely on our five senses to lead the most productive life possible, it is imperative that we focus, pay attention and when necessary, intentionally feed the senses for ultimate use.

Exercise:

There is one sense that can encompass many feelings and have a lasting effect long following its use. It's the sense of touch. This sense is not one that is widely encouraged in many correctional facilities in America, however, if both parties practice this simple exercise, the limited gratification of touch that's allowed during a detention visit can be transformed to a long-standing continued connection, long after the visit has ended.

1. *Learn the parts of your hands (finger digits, palms, nerves, etc.)*
2. *Rub your hands together and hug yourself. Let the emotions flow.*
3. *Use your energy through your hands to send emotion in your hug to your loved one through your quick embrace during an in-person visit.*
4. *Acknowledge the exchange of positive energy through your hands. Words at that beginning point of the visit become optional.*

(This exercise can be performed through a partition glass)
(go to www.peaceofhope.info for more tools on feeding your senses)

Step Outside of Yourself and Take a Good Look

The field of criminal justice is a demanding field. While going through the important motions of visiting prisons, accepting phone calls, writing letters *all while juggling personal responsibilities*, it is easy to forget to pat yourself on the back for being 'That super good person!'

Take a moment to step outside of yourself and take a look at what you're accomplishing. This will help you to keep going. This motion will also help you command the respect you deserve in this role.

There will be no demands of your time, money or energy from anyone, except those demands you allow yourself.

Very important!

Your strength of patience, work ethics and level of perseverance may be stretched during this time, yet, you remain persistent.

You are surviving the other side of the wall. That is no small task. Taking a moment to step outside of yourself allows you to recognize what others may already see, but won't say. You are awesome and generous. You are to be revered for the work you are doing!

WRITE IT ALL DOWN

Staying in the moment is less physical then mental. It is very possible to utilize your skills to stay in the moment without anyone noticing. And you can literally utilize many of the techniques in this first chapter by simply closing your eyes and forming a personal level of meditation.

However, when you elevate and document

these moments, you create a memorandum of this challenging time. It is researched that nearly 95% of those imprisoned will be eventually released (https://www.bjs.gov/content/reentry/reentry.cfm). This means that it is very likely that your role as a support person of the incarcerated will someday evolve to being a *support person of the recently released*. Pictures, videos, verbal recordings, or handwritten entries give historical content that can be referred to in the future.

Exercise:

Grab a sheet of paper and a pen right now and write down what you are thinking as you read chapter one of this book. This could be the first of many entries you'll make in your role as the support person of the imprisoned. Are you excited about getting to the next chapter? Why or why not? Is this 'how-to survive the other side of the wall' book doing you any good yet? Do you believe the future chapters will be better for your needs?

These are some of the thoughts that you might want to write down. Make sure to put a date on each entry, including the time. Soon you may notice a pattern in your writing. Mondays may be the best day of the week for you to be able to feed your senses. Perhaps Tuesdays are the days you decide to step outside of yourself and take a look. Wednesday through Saturday may been when you write it all down. Whatever your pattern becomes, keep a Journal. It's good for you and will come in handy down the road.

Create a Reminder of the Current Moments

Short Story: *The conviction of my love one weighed heavily on me for nearly two years. During those times I felt displaced and 'staying in the moment' was difficult. I tried to use the exercises mentioned, but found them difficult to complete. I realized I had no choice but to survive, so I continued on.*

With effort, I stepped outside myself. Talked to myself. Went through the motions to take care of myself and remind myself to eat. Comb my hair. Feed the fish. Water my plants. Even though I had the best support team, (Family, Friends, Church, etc.) my desire to 'survive' was minimal. Basic chores were forgettable. But since other people were dependent on me (notably my 2 younger children), I had to figure something out quick!

I decided to create reminders. I bought regular yellow sticky notes and put them on different parts of my apartment. There was a sticky note on the mirror that said 'smile'. Then there was the sticky note on the front door reminding me to brush my hair before I left to go to work. There were select pictures of me and my detained loved one throughout my place. Yes times were tough in the beginnings of my role as a support person of my incarcerated loved one and I probably should have sought mental treatment! But creating those reminders of the moment helped to bring me back to the strong person who I was raised to be.

Create reminders for yourself! Do it the way that works for you. For me it was sticky notes and pictures, for you it may be a handmade piece of art or a special letter. Create visuals that are uplifting, even something that you can touch, a paper, a pillow, something that incites good feelings in your spirit. Perhaps you have a favorite scripture. Be creative and make a reminder of the moment. You are able to do more than just exist -- you can SURVIVE and THRIVE on this side of the wall!

CHAPTER 2

Prepare Yourself for What Lies Ahead

"You can never be too prepared". This old adage is especially true when you are a support person for someone behind bars.

The first chapter of this book centered on strengthening yourself and applying those empowerment tools while surviving your love one's incarceration. Now, it's on to application.

Preparation to face what lies ahead is crucial while supporting a person who you know personally that is being detained. By practicing the aforementioned exercises, your mental preparation is being fed. However, there still remain a few practical preparations that should be adhered to during this tumultuous journey.

A number one staple of preparation as a survivor on the other side of the wall is to have, hold and keep current I.D. for yourself. While this may seem trivial to some, it is essential to almost all of the attributes necessary as a support person of the imprisoned. A valid, current I.D. also gives you a base to refer to. That is YOU on the I.D., YOUR current address and other vital information about YOU.

Your I.D. directly contradicts any common negative statement such as "I'm in prison doing time too". No you are not! You are the person on the legal I.D. you carry and the address listed is not a detention facility.

Keeping your I.D. current and handy should be a conscience goal, especially during this time. It will come in useful during times of correspondence with your detained loved one and of course in nearly all situations in life on this side of the wall.

What lies ahead as a supporter of your loved one that's incarcerated is a lot of communication. Surviving this awkward situation will require knowledge of basic logistics:

- Where is the facility located?
- Who is the warden?
- Can my person be bailed out?
- How do I visit my loved one that's imprisoned?

and other pertinent questions that will need answers. It is a relief to know the answers to these kind of questions. Less stress!

Visiting your loved one may become a large part of your new role. Visiting requires planning, preparation and paper! You have to be mentally prepared for a long drive. Most prisons are not located within inner cities. They are usually located hundreds of miles out in outlying suburbs way far away. Knowing this, visualize yourself riding along with others who are experiencing nearly exactly what you are going through.

At this point, preparing yourself for what lies ahead should include joining "Peace of Hope, Inc." (PeaceOH). This is a large part of preparation and could save you a lot of time and money. You already know you must have valid ID with you when visiting.

Next, there is an 'application to visit' form that all detention facilities adhere to, although the process varies throughout the system (see example).

SAMPLE VISITING FORM

**This is a *modified example* of the
'MN Visiting Privilege Application Form'
******DO NOT USE!!!**
Use the latest version of the authentic visitation form for your State when visiting

MINNESOTA DEPARTMENT OF CORRECTIONS

Visiting Privilege Application Form

Do not attempt to visit until notified by the offender that your application to visit has been approved. Applications can take *several weeks* to process. Your patience is appreciated. ALL AREAS OF THE APPLICATION MUST BE COMPLETED IN BLACK INK OR THE APPLICATION WILL BE REJECTED. FAXES ARE NOT ACCEPTED ALL FORMS OF COMMUNICATION ARE SUBJECT TO MONITORING The information requested on this form will be used by the institution to determine whether or not to approve you to enter the institution as a visitor. You are not legally required to provide this information, but failure to do so may result in not allowing you to enter the institution. A check with law enforcement will be made to find out whether or not you have a criminal record. Whether you are approved or not, this form will be kept on file. The result of the criminal history check is destroyed. The only persons or agencies who will have access to this information will be those who have legal access to private or confidential data maintained by the Minnesota Department of Corrections. MSA 243.55 CONTRABAND ARTICLES; EXCEPTIONS; PENALTY Subdivision 1. Any person who brings, sends, or in any manner causes to be introduced into any state correctional facility or state hospital, or within or upon the grounds belonging to or land controlled by any such facility or hospital, any controlled substance as defined in section 152.01, subdivision 4, or any firearms, weapons, or explosives of any kind, without the consent of the Warden thereof, shall be guilty of a felony and, upon conviction thereof, punished by imprisonment for a term of no less than three, nor more than five years. Any person who brings, sends, or in any manner causes to be introduced into any state correctional facility or within or upon the grounds belonging to or land controlled by the facility, any intoxicating or alcoholic liquor or malt beverage of any kind without the consent of the Warden thereof, shall be guilty of a gross misdemeanor. The provisions of this section shall not apply to physicians carrying drugs or introducing any of the above-described liquors into such facilities for use in the practice of their profession; nor to sheriffs or other peace officers carrying revolvers or firearms as such officers in the discharge of duties. All persons and their belongings entering this institution or upon the grounds thereof may be subject to search for contraband articles at any time. Admittance will be denied to anyone refusing to subject their person or belongings to a search. A Victim is prohibited to apply for visiting privileges and visiting with an offender while incarcerated. Applications for the following facilities should be sent to the address below.

All visiting applications for every facility are processed at MCF-Rush City (except Red Wing Juveniles) MCF-Rush City Attn: Visiting Unit 7600 525th Street Rush City, MN 55069 Visiting Applications for Red Wing Juveniles are sent to Red Wing MCF-Red Wing Attn: Visiting Unit 1079 Highway 292 Red Wing, MN 55066 302.100A (10/2018)

Please Print

Offender:_____

(Last, First Middle)   OID# _____

Visitor: _____
Last First Full Middle Maiden Name/Aliases

DOB: _____ Gender: _____ Address:_____

City: _____ State: _____ Zip Code: _____
Phone Number: (_____)_____

Relationship to Offender (e.g., Parent, Spouse, Friend):

_____

Anyone under 18 years of age must be escorted by a parent, legal guardian or an authorized escort A copy of each minor's state/county birth certificate must be sent with the visiting application. Birth certificates will not be accepted at the time of visit. The hospital's Heirloom Birth Certificate, or Crib Card, is not an official document and will not be accepted. If an adult other than the parent or legal guardian escorts a minor, a notarized Minor Escort Form signed by the child's custodial parent/guardian must accompany the birth certificate.

Minor's Full Name: DOB:

***If you answer yes to any question below, please explain in COMMENTS

1.   Have you ever been a resource/volunteer/employee at any MN correctional facility?
2.   Do you have ANY pending charges against you?
3.   Do you have any Non-Contact Orders or OFP's with anyone incarcerated in the DOC?
4.   Are you on another offender's visiting list at any MN correctional facility?
5.   Have you ever been released from a state or federal correctional facility?
6.   Are you on probation, parole or release status? (If yes, you must include your agent's name and/or county, and phone number below) Agent's Printed Name: _____
     Phone# (____)_____ ***COMMENTS: _____

Type of ID - Enter ID Number: **An expired/canceled Driver's License does not qualify as a valid ID for visiting purposes.**
Signature: _____   Date: _____

THE ABOVE INFORMATION IS TRUE AND CORRECT. I UNDERSTAND THAT PROVIDING FALSE INFORMATION ON THIS FORM IS GROUNDS FOR DENYING VISITING PRIVILEGES. If application is not legible, it will be denied. FOR OFFICE USE ONLY Received_____ Criminal History Check Completed on_____ Approved_____ Denied_____ Staff Initials_____ Driver's license or ID Card from state/territory of residence #:_____***Photocopy of ID or **Driver's License must be attached or application will be denied.** Valid military ID #:_____ Matricula Consular ID #:_____ Minnesota Tribal ID#_____Passport#:_____

There are several other logistical necessities involved when visiting.

Dress code is of prime importance. Read the policy and know what is expected of you during this part of your journey. Also, jail (or other detention facilities other than prisons) often have video visits only. Know the rules in your jurisdiction so you will know exactly what to expect. Contacting 'Peace of Hope, Inc.' is a smart move! Peace of Hope members are experienced. All of them have survived being on the other side of the wall or were citizens behind the wall at one point themselves. Many members, like myself, are currently still supporting several loved ones who are detained right now at the time of this writing.

Preparing for what lies ahead makes it possible to alleviate many of the stresses associated with having a loved one imprisoned.

Surviving the dilemma becomes easier.

Prepare!

Peace of Hope, Inc.

Expert Resource for Families of the Incarcerated & Reentry'd

We will help you assess your situation!

☞ Bail Bonds
☞ Court appearances
☞ Visiting information
☞ Individual Counseling
☞ And more!

Peace of Hope, Inc. est. 2012

"Expert Resource for Families of the Imprisoned & Reentry'd"

Email: contactpeaceofhope@gmail.com

Contributions Accepted at: Paypal.me/Peace of Hope

Sharon Brooks Green, CEO

Regaining Motivation

Short Story: My loved one had been jailed for 6 months. He was being held without bail for felony charges while on probation. During those 6 months I was his premier supporter. I accepted phone calls, made visits, attended court appearances and kept him abreast of the outside world. This had become part of my life. By the time he went to prison, I was drained. My motivation from the courthouse did not automatically transfer to his stay in prison. I needed help. By using tools suggested by Peace of Hope, Inc., I was not overwhelmed. I had support by them for myself to deal with this new direction in my life. 'Peace of Hope' also allowed me to share these experiences with other people in my community who were going through the same thing. My energy began to regain itself and I was able to continue in my role as support person for the next several years of my life. I'm glad I had this organization. They helped me survive the other side of the wall.

A Visiting Day in 2012, MCF-Stillwater
Me and my Son Marquis Rollins

Regaining motivation does not mean that you've ever lost motivation. It may simply mean, as outlined in the story, that you have to shift the focus of your motivation to regain the momentum again. I had to regain refocus, shift a line and level up . In doing so there were certain steps I had to take in order to achieve my goal of regaining motivation to be the best support person I could be while maintaining my own equilibrium and survival.

Here is a definite suggestion:

1.   Learn all you can about the detention facility.

My experience with having a loved one incarcerated in jail/prison was a form of higher education for me. I had to quickly learn the logistics of the prison system: Where the prison was, what a prison was, who was in charge and what did they do with 10% of the money I sent? What was my loved one allowed to do with his time while incarcerated?

There was so much to learn! Actually, pertinent information can be found on a detention center's website.

(Most state and federal prisons usually have a website and are able to be found using Google search , e.g. Minnesota Department of Corrections, https://mn.doc/gov).

There is much information to be found on a correctional facility website, such as:

- What educational benefits are available to your loved one
- Race, religion and population numbers on a daily basis
- Commissioner, Deputy Commissioner and other ranked officials
- Policy manuals
- Resources for families of the imprisoned (if provided)

It is very important for you to learn all you can about the detention facilities that your loved one is housed at. Read up on their policies! Policy interpretation can be done through Peace of Hope. You may want to go to our website and post your question to get clearer understanding on any policy.

Using these tools will help you function better on the other side of the wall.

Reaching Plateaus

Every day counts. One year, 2 years, 5 years or even 10, 20 years from now- the moment that your loved one is incarcerated, is the time to start preparing for what lies ahead upon their release. This preparation can be met more joyfully by setting goals or plateaus for yourself.

1. *Schedule every phone call and visit with your loved one.* This requires acknowledging that you are now living two very different lives from each other, with two very different sched- ules. Successful contact must be coordinated in order to be effective. *Make this a goal.* You and your loved one will have to work together to make this plateau successful. Right away you both will realize this is much easier than a 'hit or miss' phone call or visit where one or both of you are either not in the mood for company or simply unavailable. It happens.

2. *Make yourself aware of the detention facility rules and regula- tions that your loved one now lives by.* If you're both abiding by those rules and regulations and understanding the language of the policies and procedures, the less chance of violation. This goal is quite beneficial to being more mentally healthy while dealing with the fact that your loved one now lives at that facility.

CHAPTER 3

Create a New Normal

Your previous normal does not exist anymore.

This is a phenomenon that you probably already know. Everything is different: your schedule, the way you hear the news, your reaction to old pictures and even the mention of your loved one's name. This is all o.k.

It is not unusual nor is it anything to be wary of. The fact is, someone you know and care for is living behind the wall, which automatically places you on the other side. The goal of this book is to provide tools on how to survive it all, and creating a new normal will be necessary to get there.

Your new normal creates a heightened sense of awareness about you now that without a doubt may be quite noticeable by you and others.

You may have internal concerns regarding your importance of support for your loved one that's being detained. Keep that concern and use it to give yourself continual clarity on your decision to move intentionally in this role.

Your newfound 'being' consist of more patience and practicality for yourself. It has to be since your *investment* as a supporter of the imprisoned is coupled with the knowledge that you may eventually evolve to being the support person for the *reentry'd.*

Your 'new normal' includes demeanor, conversation, schedule and even lifestyle choices. Friends and associations are not to be haphazard. It becomes quite relevant to surround yourself with positivity while dealing with the fact that your loved one now lives in a detention facility.

You may have to work more hours or less. Your network dynamics have changed. The very love within yourself, for yourself has become deeper. Crying is not seen as a weakness, but a personal release of acknowledged emotions and yes, you are allowed to cry.

That said, in order to stay on the survivors path, there is one face you show to the public and there is another one that is extremely personal.

Creating this new normal gives you the strength to fight the battles you may have to fight during this time, because we all know that challenges of life do not stop or pause just because your loved one is incarcerated. In fact there are additional challenges that may occur during this phase of life. Creating and acknowledging your 'New Normal' will help you to survive whatever comes your way.

Exercise:

Take deep breaths.... Relax.... Envision yourself in your 'new normal'. See yourself as you want others to see you. When making the difficult trips to visit your loved one that's incarcerated, be the new you. Your new found strengthened way of surviving the other side of the wall will be noticeable by all, including your incarcerated loved ones. Be your new you in your day to day life. You are not a victim on the other side of the wall, but a supporter of a loved one that lives behind the wall. Take control of your new normal. Embrace it.

The next few topics give some suggestions on how to create your new normal.

Make a New Budget

In order to maintain yourself you need clear order about your money. When the person incarcerated comes directly from your household or is a close acquaintance who depends on you for support, finances become a big issue fast!

Personal budgets change. Perhaps your budget increased when your loved one was detained. Sadly, this is possible because your person behind bars is a juvenile who you were financially responsible for. And now you're not...for now.

A new personal finance budget must be made.

Another scenario could involve an adult loved one whose incarcerated, that was bringing in money. And now they are not.

In that case your personal budget has decreased and must be readjusted.

This attention to your money and how it's spent during this time will assist you greatly while surviving the other side of the wall.

Many times we may start at a deficit because of the high cost of attorneys and other fees that may have been needed during the judicial cycle. Here are steps to take to find out exactly where you are financially and deal with, even excel in, as you become the 'new you' in this dynamic involving mass incarceration.

Exercise:

1. Use a ledger. Determined what your income is at this time. Write the number and sources down (e.g. $1050/ bi-weekly from Job, $300 Food support, $100/wk Hair braiding, etc.)

2. In the ledger, determine what your expenses are at this time. Be sure to include a monthly expense you intend to use as support for your love one incarcerated (phone cost, money on their books, transportation, etc.)

22

Be realistic about this number.

And also be prepared to *not be swayed to increase this number*. Most expenses for your detained loved one are covered by the institutional facility that they are housed at. Additional income that you send to your loved one at a detention facility such as jail or prison, may be accosted a fee deducting up to 20% of your finances sent in. Keep this in mind. (e.g. $20 sent becomes $16.00) Consult the policies of the facility that your loved one is housed at.

3. Still using your ledger, allow yourself to save a minimum 3% of your income per month for emergency purposes regarding your role as support person of the imprisoned. This savings can be placed in a special account with 'Peace of Hope, Inc.' More information about the use and benefits of this savings can be requested at: contactpeaceofhope@gmail.com

Plan for Their Eventual Release

As an experienced expert in this topic, I know what you should not do upon your loved one's eventual release: Forego planning for it.

The number one thing not to do is to not plan for their eventual release.

More than likely, there will come a day when your loved one is released from the detention facility that they are at now. Although the days may seem long and you are surviving by preparing yourself and reaching plateaus, using your senses, acknowledging your thoughts, all while preparing and utilizing a new budget, it is imperative to realize that the 'new you' may someday be the support person of a formerly incarcerated person. It's extremely possible that a day may come that your loved one walks up to your door and says hello.

Are you ready?

You must plan for their eventual release. Fortunately you have the right book in your hand. What does it mean to plan for your loved one to come home from prison? How do you actually prepare for that moment? Because you have continued to live, things in your life may be different. Perhaps you've changed the house around, or maybe even have moved from the old address.

In doing so, it may appear that you have planned, however, strategic steps must be intentionally taken in order to be fully prepared for your loved ones eventual release.

1. Know the statutes of your community concerning felony restrictive rights for those to live in the community, especially if your loved one is coming to live or visit with you.

   Do not be surprised on the day of your love one's release. Know what's allowed and what's not allowed, what you will accept and what you're willing to fight for. However the day of the release is not the time to decide. Those of us who are surviving the other side of the wall, we know that the day to plan for release is on the first day of incarceration. Make sure you do your homework on this topic.

2. Refer to your Journal. The notes you have been taking become central to visualizing how the 'new them' that's returning to the 'new you' will relate. Hopefully, you've carefully written down notes that chronicled your journey. Have conversations that allow visualization of continued education, if that's what they want to do. Talk about and prepare for employment, housing, or the new neighbors with lots of pets in their yard. These are concurrent conversations to be implemented in timely fashions. As you both approach the day of release, these docu-

mented conversations should have turned into productive action work. Housing, employment and a welcoming neighborhood should all be lined up.

(Attend a "Peace of Hope" seminar in your area for more specific instructions on how to tactfully facilitate these much needed conversations). You will be asked to bring your Journal with you.

3. Together, plan how days 1, 2, and 3 of your loved one's return home will be spent. Be aware that during the initial arrival, a representative of the criminal justice system (parole agent, probation officer, police officer, etc.) may be involved. Know exactly what's expected and be prepared. Your loved one may also be placed on 'house arrest' or with limited and monitored mobility. Discuss all of the release protocols with this person who you have been supporting during their incarceration, especially if they will be returning home to live with you.

This is absolutely <u>not</u> the time to throw a wild party in celebration of your loved one's return home. It may even be wise to not have company of the 'past' stop by, as this may be a time of re-acclimation for you both and/or the entire family.

Post rules around your home, very similar to the inspirational notes you may have hung on your walls for yourself. These rules are to be abided by. There is an awesome transition that has occurred with your loved one from being housed in a cage to being housed at home with you . At the same time there is a magnificent transition that is occurring within you , from the old you to the new you to the new you that's 'becoming' as you adjust to your loved one's return home to you and the family.

Be Intentional

Incarceration has such a negative stigma around it and rightfully so. It is not a fun place to be, it is not the place to 'grow' when experiencing the normal passage to adulthood and if it should occur anyway within a family, it is not a glorious moment. It is a negative situation, one that Black people face more than 5x more likely than any other race throughout America (https://www.naacp.org/criminal-justice-fact-sheet/).

At this point, being intentional about your role of support person of the incarcerated must be accepted by you or not. When hearing statistics such as the one quoted, surviving a loved one's incarceration becomes paramount. Whether Black, Native, White, Latino, African, Asian or otherwise, there is an inherent natural instinct to give as much support as possible to our loved one who is detained.

Short story: "When I heard the judge say 127 months I immediately got out my calculator and did the math: WHAT?! 10 + years!!!!! I decided to become extremely educated during the final version of this criminal justice system process, which is prison. I utilized all of the exercises that this book has offered to you. Then, as I became stronger, I enrolled in school at Inver Hills Community College and pursued an Associate's degree in the field of Individualized Studies, focused on Advocacy for Families of the Imprisoned. This program allowed me to study classes such as 'Police & the Community', 'Criminal Justice' as well as 'Music', 'Storytelling' and 'Theater'. The latter classes reminded me of my joys in this life! The Individualized Studies program choice (same focus) continued throughout my undergraduate journey at Metro State University in MN, where I pursued and obtained a B.A Degree. My focus included courses such as 'The Rehabilitation of the Public Offender', 'Constitutional Law', 'Music', 'Storytelling' and 'Theater'. During my entire educational journey I was able to talk freely about my love one's incarceration. By this time I was into year 3 as the main supporter. The joy of learning and the ability to talk about my role really helped me identify how intentional I was about being the support person of my loved one who was imprisoned. I formed 'Peace of Hope' (PeaceOH) during this time and excelled at showing others how to be intentional in this unique role of support. Eventually, supporting my loved one involved entering the political realm with a bill that supported supporters like myself! Two versions of this bill were proposed and written by me in 2018 & 2019 (with support from the MN D.O.C. administration in 2018).

I am very grateful that MN Representative Raymond Dehn authored both proposals. They are called 'The Peace of Hope Transit Bills". "The Peace of Hope Transit" Bills HF 4151 & 1518 respectively, were created to remove barriers of visitation for loved ones of the imprisoned. Co-authors of the bills included Rep. Lyndon Carlson, Rep. Fue Lee, (then) Rep. Ilhan Omar, Rep. Rena Moran, Sen. Bobby Joe Champion and Sen. Jeff Hayden. During this time I was finishing MAPL (Masters of Advocacy & Political Leadership) Graduate school at Metro State University, MN.

I had applied and been accepted to the MN Task Force for Justice Involved Women and Girls, a role I currently serve in. I also continue as facilitator and co-planner for Metro State's popular annual forum "Understanding and Responding to Mass Incarceration" (URMI). My loved one who had been detained for too many years was now released, and along with his little sister Kamouri (PeaceOH Top Chef) and younger brother Lawrence (PeaceOH Analyst), we began to work together on issues concerning support for families of the imprisoned & reentry'd. That work continues today.

Facilitators Mr. Marquis Rollins & Me
MN D.O.C.- Strengthening Families of the Incarcerated, Spring 2018

You've invested a lot of time, money, energy and even access to this person's life and allowed them into yours. Your intentionality of support and how it is discussed about your loved one is contagious.

I've allowed others to freely discuss their own feelings about incarceration with me. I've intentionally opened the door to this 'stigma' that in many arenas was previously nailed shut. You too with your 'new normal', with your new confidence, with the way you're handling the finances, the way you've continued on ---are now able to openly and proactively support your loved one that's incarcerated and survive being on this other side of the wall. Yes, be intentional.

Establish Routine

There are plenty of assumptions about those of us who are predict-able. In my world I prefer routine. Ask yourself, are you predict-able? Do you always have a cup of coffee in the morning? Can you be depended upon to be at the bus stop at exactly 6:15 AM and greet the same people everyday ? On Saturdays, is the neighbor's dog barking because the paper is delivered at 5am and you know that's the reason for the bark? They're some things we all have a routine with and that is not entirely a bad thing. Routine helps keep us grounded. Now that you've claimed control of yourself , not of the situation, but of yourself, how you respond to it must be with the highest wisdom. Routine can help establish that. Now that you've establish a new normal, it may be time for a new routine.

Your role as the support person of an imprisoned loved one may demand that you get a new routine. You are scheduling phone calls, scheduling visits, determining how much money can or cannot be spent each month, you are the CEO of this demonstration! Yes, your loved one's role is not diminished, but this side of the wall is your domain. You map out the way you choose what determines you as a survivor of living on the other side of the wall. A new routine may likely be in order.

Exercise:

Get a binder in your favorite color. This is not the same binder as the ledger you use for the budgeting. This is the binder you use for scheduling. It will be changed, updated, fixed, scratched out, high-lighted and everything else until you find a new routine that fits your new normal. This binder is personal, but keep it in a location that you can look at and internalize it's content. Remember, any and all alterations you make on the pages of the binder are the perfect changes for you. Establish your routine to fit the new you.

29

CHAPTER 4

What to Tell the Children

C hildren are little *people.* A whole person possessing all of their senses coupled with honesty, dependency and trust. Many of these little people come with faculties equal to what we call 'old souls'. What to tell the children about your intentional role as the support person of someone they know that's now imprisoned? This answer must be decided by you BEFORE it becomes an issue.

There are many times a child won't need to know information concerning very serious issues during the development of this situation such as court dates, etc. However, if detention should occur, some level of knowledge about it must be shared with the children. News such as this should be delivered by you, not the media or others. *With you as the decider, a child's school may need to be alerted of the drastic change that has occurred in the child's life.* Children are an intricate part of the family network. It is essential to include them in the level of conversation you gauge that they can handle. It is also best not to deeply bombard them with details. A simple explanation may be "Dad won't live with us for a while he has to stay in a prison now". Allow the child to figure out how he wants to process that information . Depending on the age, the 1st question may not be "What is a prison?" but may be the more popular universal children's question of "Why?" That is where you need to decide your tactic.

Exercise:

Choose your location that you will deliver this information.

1. Let it be a comfort zone for you both. A place you all are familiar with and can communicate easily: McDonald's, The local park, or maybe even at the kitchen table (this works well with adults). You chose who you tell. Be at peace as to why you've decided to share this information with this person. Choosing the setting will give you more empowerment in your delivery, but young or old, you cannot choose their response. Allow natural questions and emotions to rule. A more honest outcome will be at hand.

2. Remember to practice your own survival techniques learned in earlier chapters of this book. Those tools will help you maintain your new normal as you receive the response from the person you've entrusted this information to.

3. Children may not ask ALL of their questions right then and there. Expect them to come back later with just one more question or even a day or two later with a few more. Be patient. Build them up and eventually, when or if you decide, the occasion to visit your imprisoned loved one with the children will go much more smoothly.

Short Story: *In Spring 2018, I was approached by a generous group of attorneys who wanted to lend support to children of incarcerated caregivers. Together we decided to facilitate transportation for these children to visit their caregivers in detention facilities, primarily female prisons. My method of attracting these children was to partner with a locally known children's musical story-teller 'Mr. Cleanhouse and Friends'. Through our combined efforts, "Mr. Cleanhouse" dressed in his 'Afro G' character, told musical stories of a boy named Kobe whose father had been arrested and eventually imprisoned. Kobe had many point-of-views. Our weekly growing audience, ages 5-15, loved the on-going story! We served yummy frozen yogurt and delicious pizza. In return, the children had lively visits with their incarcerated care-givers for the next year while continuing to actively participate with the story-telling with us throughout the Summer. We made the tough topic of imprisonment relatable for the children. Awesome!*

Summer 2018
Children's Musical Story-Teller "Mr. Cleanhouse"
(www.mr.cleanhouse.com) and Peace of Hope,
Inc. at *Cherry Berry* in Minnesota

CHAPTER 5

You Survived Your Loved One's Incarceration

L et's begin with the end in mind.

From day one that your loved one is arrested and placed into a detention center, that is the day that you begin to prepare for your loved one's eventual release from imprisonment. That means preparing yourself with strength, stability and a new normal. This will require unshakeable belief in faith and in yourself.

You have equipped yourself with armors of available education. You know where to find the policies and procedures of the facility that is holding your loved one as a 'client'. You have decided what you will accept and what you will advocate to change. You have also equipped yourself with 'senses building exercises' that you can use to keep yourself elevated.

The binder(s) in your favorite color work to keep your new and sometimes changing routine on track. Use a ledger for your budget and know exactly where you are financially.

Live intentionally in this new role.

This feeling of strength may be transferred over to the loved one who you are supporting, making it easier to mutually agree on a schedule of phone calls, visits and how finances will be distributed during this time of real transformation.

Because of this, you can grow together. There is mutual motivation. When release date approaches, a new respect for the new you would have been developed. In the event of no release date in sight, a growing bond may have been re-established.

You are unashamed, guilt free and in preparation for your role as the support person of the incarcerated.

Your support continues through the reentry process and a decision for where they return may or may not include sharing living space with you. You are ready to weigh the many options of reentry and not be desperate for situations that are not mutually beneficial for both parties.

You will consult your journals and be honest about your supportive actions and the way in which they were received. You will remain strong as you seek further guidance and assistance with 'Peace of Hope" and other resources that provide support for supporters of the incarcerated.

You have survived the other side of the wall. You have hope.

Exercise:

1. This book was designed on purpose as a convenient sized paperback for quick referral. Carry it with you. Write in it. Highlight entries. Make it your own. Points that speak directly to you - circle or dog ear the entire page. Obtain a copy of this book for a friend.

2. Give yourself a hand! You are officially surviving the other side of the wall! Sign on with 'Peace of Hope' and let us know your thoughts about this handbook by Sharon Brooks Green. (Send your thoughts to contactpeaceofhope@gmail.com).

3. Share the wealth of knowledge! At 'Peace of Hope' we have a need for those who are survivors of their loved ones incarceration and have utilized 'Peace of Hope's' principles to do so (those that are found in this book, etc.). Find out how you can become a voice in your community as a representative of 'Peace of Hope' while offering words of wisdom of how to successfully survive the other side of the wall. Go to www. peaceofhope.info and sign up today.

Conclusion

Truly, the saga of having a loved one in prison doesn't have to end your joy, but causes a reach for deeper meaning, deeper strength. You read "The Other Side of the Wall: How to Survive your Loved One's Incarceration" in full and are empowered in a variety of ways!

Thank you for buying this book, for finishing this book, but most importantly, for trusting the content. I appreciate that what you will do as you step outside that door now as a survivor of the other side of the wall, will make an impact on how you respond to the many situations that often occur when your loved one is detained.

I welcome you to contact me. Send me your review and let me know what portion of this book assisted you the most. What was the best part for you? Was it creating your 'new normal', 'journaling' or perhaps 'staying in the moment'? Let me know!

You are also welcome to become a member at "Peace of Hope" (www.peaceofhope.info) . We look forward to you joining our team in assisting us in helping the next person survive the other side of the wall.

Lastly, I'd like to introduce you to Peace of Hope's logo. The thick Peace sign in the middle represents the countless numbers of detention facilities in the world that hold human souls captive. The peace sign is enclosed within the Sun, the most powerful star in the universe. Our star of Hope. The Vibrant rays beaming from the Sun are you and me. With strength from our Star, we the family, friends, loved ones and others, are enriched with peace and hope to survive on the other side of the wall.

Made in the USA
Coppell, TX
03 October 2020

39184727R00029